CROOKED CROWNS ARE PERFECT

(A Self-Worth Guide for Teen Girls and Women)

CROOKED CROWNS ARE PERFECT

(A Self-Worth Guide for Teen Girls and Women)

Copyright © 2023 by Tanda J. Canion. All rights reserved.

No part of this book may be reproduced or transmitted in any form or by any means, electronic or mechanical, including photocopying, recording, or by any information storage and retrieval system without permission in writing from the publisher.

All references are from the Holy Bible's New King James Version (NKJV).

Printed and manufactured in the United States of America.

Registered with the Library of Congress.

First Edition: 2023

TABLE OF CONTENT

INTRODUCTION 5
IN THE BEGINNING 9
TWISTED IMAGE 13
WHY SELF-WORTH IS IMPORTANT 17
FEARFULLY AND WONDERFULLY MADE 23
PERFECTIONIST 29
PHOTOSHOPPED 33
THE MEAN GIRL SYNDROME 39
BLACK SHEEP 43
THE LOWDOWN ON GETTING REJECTED 49
BROKE PEARLS 53
FAILURE IS NOT AN OPTION 57
GAME CHANGER 61
CONFIDENCE BOOSTER 67
17 WAYS TO OVERCOME LOW SELF-ESTEEM 71
YOU ARE STRONGER THAN YOU KNOW 85
CREATE THE LIFE YOU WANT TO LIVE 89
WOMEN OF THE BIBLE WITH CROOKED CROWNS 95
INSPIRATIONAL QUOTES 97
CROOKED CROWN AFFIRMATIONS 101
WORKSHEET 1 105
WORKSHEET 2 111
EPILOGUE 115
MEET THE AUTHOR 117

INTRODUCTION

Hey, fabulous readers! Welcome to "Crooked Crowns Are Perfect. The ultimate self-esteem book that's all about embracing our uniqueness and celebrating the fantastic individuals we are. In this book, we will journey together to discover the beauty in our differences and learn to wear our crooked crowns with pride.

We live in a society whose emphasis is on the outward appearance instead of the true beauty within. The measure of a woman has moved from inner beauty to shaming her for the wonderful qualities given to her by God at birth. Race, size, shape, and status have become the rules by which she is measured. These unattainable expectations have forced girls and women to aspire to perfection and devalue who they are inside.

Focusing on outward appearance should not be the primary concern; we want to break free from the idea that our value is based on looks, which can make you feel like you are not enough. The pressure to be perfect has led many girls and women to set unrealistically high expectations for themselves, forgetting to celebrate the awesome people they are.

Billions of dollars are spent annually on girls and women aiming to change their appearance because standards have been set by people who do not value their worth. Not only have these practices become a money game, but it has also created emotional trauma in girls who do not look to part according to their standards.

Everyone wants to be their best version, and self-improvement is absolutely nothing wrong. Still, when those improvements affect your mental, physical, emotional, and spiritual health, it is not worth it.

My Granddaughter, Lyric was born with a certain grace that she carries given to her by God. I recognized it and started cultivating what I saw. It was unimportant for her to enter pageants because the photos I had seen in that sport were not inviting for little girls. It felt like pressure for them to be perfect. Out of nowhere, invitations came in the mail, but they all went to the trash, unknown to us; God had another plan for our lyrics.

I was afforded the wonderful opportunity to assist our granddaughter, Lyric, as she navigated the world of pageantry and became a State Beauty Queen, national competitor, and runner-up in several categories within the system. Long practices, budgets, travel, gorgeous gowns, tailored clothes, discipline, and fierce competition became our lives during pageant season. It was all worth it because we saw her shine on the stage like the light she was born to be. The pageant system aimed to help girls develop confidence, build life skills, and cultivate life-long friendships. I loved that system because the emphasis was not on outer beauty and make-up, and swimwear was forbidden at a certain age. Girls of all sizes, races, and personalities won despite physical limitations.

Lyric's pageant journey started in elementary school when her teacher nominated her. Many girls were gorgeous and well deserved the elementary school title. To our surprise, Lyric became the elementary school queen after one attempt at the title. Our family was overtaken with joy as she stood on the stage confidently in her abilities.

Lyric was gorgeous, but I noticed her crown was crooked. I quickly attempted to make my way to the stage to correct it, but it was too late because the cameras flashed as she posed with her trophies, awards, and crooked crown. I emphasized the crown sitting perfectly on her head instead of being present. I shifted my attitude because it did not matter how crooked the crown was; it could not tarnish that precious moment she was crowned and eradicate the fact that she was still the elementary school queen. We could not have been prouder of her, and the crooked crown was perfect.

Life is not about fitting into someone else's idea of perfect; it is about recognizing that our quirks, imperfections, and unique qualities make us extraordinary. Just like crowns, which come in all shapes and sizes, our self-esteem should shine brightly, no matter how crooked or unconventional it may seem.

This book aims to empower girls and women to let up on themselves because no one is perfect but the big guy upstairs. He alone stands in that category, and the rest of us must accept our fallen nature as the cause of our imperfections. God skillfully and wonderfully made you, and He loves you unconditionally the way you are.

Prepare for a delightful adventure filled with positivity, self-love, and the realization that each of us is skillfully and wonderfully made. ," the ultimate self-esteem book that's all about celebrating our uniqueness. In these pages, we are on a journey together to find beauty in our differences and learn to rock our crooked crowns confidently.

So, let's dive in and uncover the magic of our crooked crowns because, in this book, imperfection is not just okay – it's perfect!

Father, as I read this book, open my eyes and heart to embrace who I am in you. Help me to become the best version of myself so I may be light and pleasing to you.

IN THE BEGINNING

¹ In the beginning, God created the heavens and the earth.

² Now the earth was formless and empty, darkness was over the surface of the deep, and the Spirit of God was hovering over the waters.

³ And God said, "Let there be light," and there was light.

⁴ God saw that the light was good, and he separated the light from the darkness.

⁵ God called the light "day," and the darkness he called "night." And there was evening, and there was morning—the first day.

⁶ And God said, "Let there be a vault between the waters to separate water from water."

⁷ So God made the vault and separated the water under the vault from the water above it. And it was so.

⁸ God called the vault "sky." And there was evening, and there was morning—the second day.

⁹ And God said, "Let the water under the sky be gathered to one place, and let dry ground appear." And it was so.

¹⁰ God called the dry ground "land," and the gathered waters he called "seas." And God saw that it was good.

[11] Then God said, "Let the land produce vegetation: seed-bearing plants and trees on the land that bear fruit with seed in it, according to their various kinds." And it was so.

[12] The land produced vegetation: plants bearing seed according to their kinds and trees bearing fruit with seed in it according to their kinds. And God saw that it was good.

[13] And there was evening, and there was morning—the third day.

[14] And God said, "Let there be lights in the vault of the sky to separate the day from the night and let them serve as signs to mark sacred times, and days and years,

[15] and let them be lights in the vault of the sky to give light on the earth." And it was so.

[16] God made two great lights—the greater light to govern the day and the lesser light to govern the night. He also made the stars.

[17] God set them in the vault of the sky to give light on the earth.

[18] to govern the day and the night, and to separate light from darkness. And God saw that it was good.

[19] And there was evening, and there was morning—the fourth day.

[20] And God said, "Let the water teem with living creatures, and let birds fly above the earth across the vault of the sky."

[21] So God created the great creatures of the sea and every living thing with which the water teems and that moves about in it, according to

their kinds, and every winged bird according to its kind. And God saw that it was good.

²² God blessed them and said, "Be fruitful and increase in number and fill the water in the seas, and let the birds increase on the earth."

²³ And there was evening, and there was morning—the fifth day.

²⁴ And God said, "Let the land produce living creatures according to their kinds: the livestock, the creatures that move along the ground, and the wild animals, each according to its kind." And it was so.

²⁵ God made the wild animals according to their kinds, the livestock according to their kinds, and all the creatures that move along the ground according to their kinds. And God saw that it was good.

²⁶ Then God said, "Let us make mankind in our image, in our likeness, so that they may rule over the fish in the sea and the birds in the sky, over the livestock and all the wild animals,[a] and over all the creatures that move along the ground."

²⁷ So God created mankind in his image, in the image of God, he created them; male and female, he created them.

²⁸ God blessed them and said to them, "Be fruitful and increase in number; fill the earth and subdue it. Rule over the fish in the sea and the birds in the sky and over every living creature that moves on the ground."

²⁹ Then God said, "I give you every seed-bearing plant on the face of the whole earth and every tree that has fruit with seed in it. They will be yours for food.

³⁰ And to all the beasts of the earth and all the birds in the sky and all the creatures that move along the ground—everything that has the breath of life in it—I give every green plant for food." And it was so.

³¹ God saw all that he had made, and it was very good. And there was evening, and there was morning—the sixth day.

God's holy word is the final authority in our lives, and it is very clear that everything made by Him was good, including you, and He was intentional about that. Once you accept God's word, your life will be transformed, and you will begin to realize how beautiful, powerful, and blessed you are.

Father, from the foundation of the world, you created me in your image. Please help me become a reflection of you. Grant me the wisdom to apply the principles you have established for my life.

TWISTED IMAGE

On the last day of creation, according to Genesis 1:27, God created man (You) in His image and finished His work with a "personal touch." God formed Adam from the dust and gave him life by sharing His breath. Humanity is unique among all God's creations, having both a material body and an immaterial soul/spirit.

This scriptural passage does not mean that God is a human, but humans are in the image of God in their moral, spiritual, and intellectual nature. Having the "image" or "likeness" of God means, in the simplest terms, that we were made to resemble God morally, spiritually, and intellectually. Adam did not resemble God in the sense of God's having his physical body. Scripture says that "God is Spirit," and He does not have a body. Adam's body was created in perfect health, and it was never in the plan of God for man to die but to live with Him forever.

The image of God is the part of man that no one can see, like his spirit and heart. This sets human beings apart from the animal world, gives them the dominion God intended them to have over the earth, and gives them a connection with God mentally, morally, and socially. Here are some examples.

Mentally, man was created as an intelligent being like God. Man can think for themselves and make free will choices. Making daily choices is an example of our being made in God's image.

Morally, man was created in righteousness without sin, and he/she was holy like God. God saw all He had made and called it "very good." Whenever someone has good behavior or feels guilty about not doing good to please God, he or she confirms that we are made in God's image.

Socially, man was created for fellowship with God, but He made the first woman because "it is not good for the man to be alone." When you make new friendships and family connections, it shows the fact that we are made in the likeness of God.

Part of being made in God's image is that Adam could make free choices. Adam and Eve made an evil choice to rebel against God. Because they did this, they were kicked out of the Garden of Eden, and they began to have a twisted image, and they passed that damaged thinking on to us. Today, we struggle to overcome the scars of sin mentally, morally, socially, and physically, which left us with twisted thinking about ourselves.

Because man disobeyed God, Satan began to rejoice because man had fallen from God, and he began to lie to us about who we are. He filled our lives with guilt, shaming, jealousy, envy, low self-esteem, bad body images, negative thoughts, and so much more.

Satan uses situations to distort our view of who we are. It is all an attack on your self-esteem. He does not want you to discover the beauty and power you possess. How you are seen is up to you because the greatest enemy is within you. How you see yourself is important. Do you take on the image of God? What causes this distortion of how you feel about yourself? Do you believe what God said about you, or do you embody the negativity of others? Sometimes, the hand we are dealt in life can give us a very bleak perspective on ourselves. A low view of ourselves causes us to see John 3:16, which reminds us of that God so loves us that He gave His only begotten Son, Jesus, as a lie.

Satan understands we were made in the image of God, so his main job has been to twist your view of yourself and others. Satan is a crafty liar who will never have your status, so he uses people, situations, and circumstances to twist your views of who you are.

The good news is that God redeemed us by sending His only begotten son, Jesus Christ, to save us and renew our minds from this twisted thinking of ourselves. Jesus is the true image of God. He restored the original image of God and created a "new self-image for us once we accept Him as the Lord of our lives (2 Corinthians 5:17).

In the beginning, you were God's final and best creation, and it is time for you to open your eyes to the lies Satan has used to twist your views of who you are; realize how beautiful you are and begin to live a life of wholeness through the renewing of your mind.

Father, I reject the lies of Satan because he is the father of lies. I rebuke all Satanic forces against my body and mind. I am who you say I am; I can be who you say I can be; and I can have what you say I can have.

WHY SELF-WORTH IS IMPORTANT

Self-worth is a sensitive topic and a very important one at that. It helps you think the way God thinks about you, and it helps you live in the purpose for which you were created. A healthy sense of self-worth can improve relationships, work, health, and overall mental and emotional well-being. If you think you might have low self-esteem, there are steps you can take to improve it and have a more positive view of yourself. After all, how we think about ourselves plays a gigantic role in every aspect of our lives.

Self-worth matters because it determines how you think and act, ultimately influencing your life's outcome. So, let's look at what it means, how to recognize it, and most importantly, how you can improve yours.

When you ask people what they think self-worth is, they probably give a shallow answer and describe what they do for a living, school activities, or what they have been graced to accomplish.

Many feel worthy if they acquire material gain, popularity, power, or likes on social media with the imposter syndrome. None of the accomplishments satisfies a person who feels unworthy.

Others who know their worth may live a simpler life, happy, peaceful, and content with what they have. I am unsure by their idea of self-worth, but you must get value from the one who gave it, Jesus Christ. Colossians 2:10 reminds us that we are complete in Him.

You must love yourself because He loved you first. He thought you were worth enough to give His life, according to John 3:16, For God so loved the world that He gave His only begotten son. You must see yourself as God sees you.

People who have a healthy sense of self-worth do not love themselves because of external metrics like:

- Grades
- Income
- Physical appearance
- Status, or title
- Occupation
- Age
- Social Media Following
- Number of real-life friends

Or any other external factor – any other factor subject to other people's perception, judgment, or opinion.

People with a healthy sense of self-worth base their love on the fact that they are humans. Lovable and valuable despite their imperfections and shortcomings because the true definition of self-worth is internal and intrinsic.

It is not about becoming self-centered but realizing that you are as valuable as the next person despite having a different upbringing, status, etc. Knowing this helps you love yourself, believe you can do anything, and be anything despite the odds.

The problem with defining self-worth based on anything external is that those measures are fleeting. The Bible says in James 4:14 that you do not know what your life will be like tomorrow. You are just a vapor that appears for a little while and then disappears.

Life is unpredictable. At one point or another, you might lose your job, go broke, lose friends, lose status, lose fans, and grow old. What then happens when any of these situations occur? Do you become less worthy or valuable?

That is the problem with basing self-worth on anything external, even if it is something you are extremely proud of. Love for oneself needs to be built on a firm foundation.

And that is why self-worth should be about you and not what you measure up to, not what other people consider success or failure.

In relationships, people with low self-worth tend to compensate by going for people they think can do what they cannot; they become dependent. They look for someone who appears inferior to them, which can shallowly boost their ego. Both combinations can lead to toxic relationships.

In professional life, people with good self-worth often take on challenging tasks because they believe they can be anything. They believe in the contributions they can make to the company.

People with healthy self-worth generally understand that they are flawed but love themselves. This means they're realistic about their expectations of themselves and others and don't mind failing.

They are not delusional but are rather able to separate their worth from results, results which are, most times, out of our total control.

How can you improve self-worth?

Improving self-worth is all about expressing unconditional love and doing your best. This means to give yourself the grace to try and fail and try again till you succeed. The result does not dent your worth or define who you are. Nothing beats an effort but a failure to try.

You need to realize that loving yourself is as simple as transferring the amount of care and attention you give to others to yourself. It means you must trust yourself and your decisions along the way.

You must love yourself enough to accept that your decisions and actions were the "best" choices you could make based on your current position. This is crucial because when others decide for you, you feel out of control and less important. You must learn to decide, stick with the decision, and be bold enough to accept the consequences of your decisions.

All this boils down to changing the inner voice in your head. It is about accepting yourself for who you are and your capabilities.

In a nutshell, you can start improving your feeling of self-worth by:

- Engaging in positive affirmations
- Accepting compliments
- Stopping the habit of self-criticism and self-loathing
- Staying away from toxic people
- Keeping track of your achievements and accomplishments

Practicing all of these will eventually improve your self-worth over time. Be patient and give yourself time to grow.

Father, you have declared me worthy and joint heirs with Christ. You saw my worth and gave your only begotten son, Jesus Christ, for me. Help me to see myself as you see me.

FEARFULLY AND WONDERFULLY MADE

Fearfully and wonderfully made speaks to the care and attention with which God has made you; you are different and unique. Never doubt how wonderful you are. You will always walk in defeat if you do not know how much God has invested in you.

Low self-esteem is defined as lacking self-confidence or seeing yourself as unworthy, inadequate, incompetent, unacceptable, or unlovable. It devalues how fearfully and wonderfully made you are by the hands of God. Self-esteem is the opinion we have of ourselves. When we have healthy self-esteem, we tend to feel positive about ourselves and about life in general. It makes us better able to deal with life's ups and downs. When our self-esteem is low, we tend to see ourselves and our lives in a more negative and critical light. If someone doesn't love themselves, they won't be motivated to take care of themselves or even accomplish much.

Ultimately, it is an attack from Satan on your identity given to you by God. If a person does not feel loved and valued, they may start to doubt themselves, their abilities, and their self-worth. In most cases, low self-esteem is usually learned. This implies that those inadequate feelings of self-worth you are experiencing were taught to you by someone else, and you started to focus on negative thoughts about yourself.

Experiences shape your thoughts and self-image unless God changes them. You see, there were adverse circumstances before you and I entered this world that caused problems before we were born; it is called sin. However, the effects of low self-esteem typically start in infancy, but with the help of the Lord, you will overcome it. Many different things can cause low self-esteem in youth, such as fitting in at school, having problems meeting your parents' expectations, and feeling unsupported, neglected, or abused; this can lead a person to feel bad about themselves.

In my book "Blood on the Floor," I discussed my upbringing in abuse and abject poverty in my childhood, which could have handicapped me for life had I chosen to allow them to. The good news is that God gave me the fortitude and wherewithal to overcome the pain of the past, and I fought to overcome low self-esteem. He also showed me that regardless of the adverse situations in life, I am an overcomer, and so are you.

Having negative, self-critical thoughts can affect your behavior and your life choices and leave you trapped in a lonely vicious circle. Stressful life events such as relationship breakdown, health issues, financial trouble, and other problems in life are contributors. Low self-esteem can also affect your quality of life and mental health, leading to stress, depression, and eating disorders. Negative feelings about yourself can translate into anxiety or depression, and this can impact the relationship you have with yourself and others.

Survivors of many different forms of trauma, such as life-threatening accidents/events, sexual abuse, and trauma, typically have low self-esteem. Before trauma, individuals usually believe in their ability to exercise good judgment and stay safe. However, after a traumatic experience, much of that trust is destroyed, which can leave a person to feel doubt, fear, helplessness, shame, and a feeling they are to blame, all eroding self-esteem.

The American Psychological Association said that women are twice as likely to develop following a traumatic event than men. Women are more commonly exposed to high-impact trauma (sexual trauma) than men at a younger age, which causes them to suffer from low self-esteem.

Self-esteem also suffers at the hands of emotional trauma, which might include incidences of harassment or such as neglect, verbal abuse, an alcoholic parent, or parental separation. The trauma of a really bad relationship, divorce, an abusive boss, or an extremely humiliating experience can scar self-esteem, too.

Some people affected by stigmas turn to other things to cope; for others, it can be polarizing and chip away at their self-esteem. Stigmas are a set of negative or unfair beliefs that a society or group of people have about something or someone. It is especially common for women, who are more likely to be stigmatized than men. Being seen as inferior because of your size, race, or religion is discrimination. These stigmas weigh heavily on people that you love: coworkers, professionals, friends, and teachers. Stigmas are effective because we might believe it is true, blaming ourselves for being stigmatized rather than the person who was unkind to us.

How can you overcome these things? First, recognize them, but you do not have to let them hurt you or accept them. You can develop coping skills to counter negative feelings, so you do not turn to other things in response. One way to counter the effects of harmful feelings is to bring to light the times when your feelings are hurt, then use your reality check and dismiss the negative thoughts that result from those negative feelings. This process can help you create a new line of thinking that leads you away from shame or negativity towards helpful thoughts.

If you have been affected by how someone views or thinks about you or called a hurtful name because of your weight, ethnicity, financial status, or social status, then you need to reimagine who you are. What you think determines how you feel, and how you feel determines what you do. Half the battle of overcoming low self-esteem is about being in the right frame of mind. It is not just about looking beautiful; it is about shifting the way you think because if you think differently, you will act differently. A shift in your mindset will help you gain greater self-awareness to make different choices to achieve your goals and become a happier, healthier person. You shift, strengthen your resilience, keep yourself motivated, make better choices, and keep going when the going gets tough.

Low self-esteem will show up in several ways. Here are some of the most common signs:

- Feeling unworthy of being loved
- Looking at the world through a negative lens
- Lack of confidence
- Fear of failure
- Perfectionism
- Difficulty hearing criticism or positive feedback from people who love you.
- Focusing on your weaknesses instead of your strengths
- Worry
- People pleasing
- Difficulty identifying and expressing your needs.
- Are you worried about how others perceive you?
- Feelings of anxiety, depression, shame, or inadequacy

If you suffer from low self-esteem, you may wonder if overcoming it and building confidence is possible. Well, the good news is that, yes, it is possible. Overcoming low self-esteem is a process that takes a lot of time and patience. Of course, there will be times when you feel like there is no change or you are wasting your time. There will also be moments when you will give up, but do not let these moments stop you. Stand up to life situations no matter how hard they seem, and in the end, you will achieve your goals and live a happy life because you deserve it.

When these feelings of low self-esteem occur, it is important to take quick action when you realize that you or someone you love is suffering from this painful problem. You can begin confronting low self-esteem and eliminating the effects of it with positive affirmations because life and death are in the power of your tongue.

So, to change this bad learned behavior, you must start learning new ones and understanding that nobody is perfect. Remind yourself of all the great attributes that God has given you. Accentuate the positive and eliminate the negative in your life, and you will begin to be all that God intended you to be. Call forth the author, the business owner, and the leader inside you. Begin to be good to yourself, making investments just as you would a close friend; you are all you have. What are you saying about yourself?

You can build self-esteem by writing down all your good qualities. You can ask someone you trust about your good qualities and not your negative ones and write down a list of good habits you have. Begin to see how detailed God created you and embrace the truth of how fearfully and wonderfully made you are.

Father, as I walk the journey of healing from low self-esteem, I thank you for allowing me to see the qualities you have given me. I pull down every stronghold that exalts itself against the knowledge of God, and I walk in the fullness of who I am.

PERFECTIONIST

What is a perfectionist? Perfectionism is the tendency to set excessively high standards for yourself and others. Some perfectionists can achieve high levels of success because of the goals they strive to meet. Others struggle with low self-esteem and problems in daily functioning when they make mistakes. Many of the goals set by a perfectionist are unrealistic and not practical. They are quick to find fault, excessively judgmental, or disapprove of themselves and others, and they tend to procrastinate out of their fear of failure. Many forget to celebrate their success because they continuously strive to improve things. Perfectionist usually makes a mountain out of a molehill.

Perfectionists refuse to accept themselves and set unrealistic expectations for themselves and others. They quickly find fault and overly criticize mistakes out of their fear of failure. They forget to celebrate small achievements while focusing on bigger ones and craving approval.

Perfectionism can be tough; it's like always aiming for an impossible standard and being too hard on us. The pressure to look a certain way has led to a billion-dollar industry, making girls feel they must change their appearance. But it's not worth it when self-improvement starts affecting our mental, physical, emotional, and spiritual health.

Childhood trauma can contribute to a perfectionist attitude if a parent or caregiver withholds love or affection. Children are likely to develop the belief that they must work hard by proving themselves or their self-worth to gain love and approval.

Perfectionists constantly strive to perform, but that can be exhausting if it is not corrected because that person sees their self-worth tied to what they achieve instead of who they are. They believe others judge them on their performance, and they can never line up to the standards they set for themselves.

In the eyes of a perfectionist, making mistakes means they are a failure or a horrible person for disappointing others or themselves. No one can live up to unrealistic expectations a perfectionist sets, and neither can they. This can lead to major control issues that sabotage relationships.

Let go of the idea of being perfect or having things perfect always because it was impossible to achieve. Everyone has flaws, including those who think that they do not. Perfectionism and the desire to be an overachiever also indicate low self-esteem. We all have gifts, but no one can be good at everything. You must put in your best efforts and leave the rest to God. He loves you so much, even with your flaws, that He died for you. Greater love hath no man than this, that He would lay down His life for His friends.

The Bible gives us the answer to this kind of attitude. There is liberty and joy that comes from humbly knowing that apart from the work of Jesus Christ in our lives, we cannot do anything of value or worth before him. Our work and best efforts are in vain if they do not please the Lord.

Crowns are shiny and heavily embellished, but they are not perfect. Many are chipped, nicked, tarnished, dented, or missing stones; however, that does not change its purpose. We are imperfect, but God has a purpose for every broken, fragmented part of our lives.

To many, the value of the crown is deducted for defects, but that is not how God sees it. II Corinthians 4:7 says, "But we have this treasure in our earthen vessel (failures, frailty, and yes, our sins), that the excellency of the power may be of God, not of us. Our imperfections magnify our need for Him and bring Him glory through our brokenness.

Imperfections in our crowns are magnified on an individual basis. Life happens to everyone regardless of their social or economic status because God designed it that way to keep us coming to Him. Within each of us is the propensity to believe we are self-made, self-taught, and self-sufficient when it is clear in Acts 17:28 that in Him, we live, move, and have our being. Our imperfections become perfect in Christ because our values come from God.

God wants you to let go of perfectionism by accepting the flaws of yourself and others and choosing to love them and yourself. God is glorified as you submit to this process of spiritual growth. He will bless you and show you favor as you seek Him for help.

Ten ways to overcome perfectionism:

1. Become more aware of it.
2. Focus on the positive instead of the negative.
3. Accept your flaws.
4. Set reasonable goals.
5. Learn to receive constructive criticism.
6. Lower the pressure you put on yourself.
7. Face your fears head-on.
8. Remember how much God loves you.
9. Allow yourself to make mistakes.
10. Laugh at your mistakes because we all make them.

Father, there is none perfect except you. I cease to pressure myself to be perfect in this human body, but I will become like you with the Holy Spirit's help. I present my body as a living sacrifice, holy and acceptable to you.

PHOTOSHOPPED

Our granddaughter, Lyric, has always had a bubbly personality, naturally poised and graceful without much effort. God gifted her with an infectious personality that always landed her out front in some capacity. She has never been frightened like other kids and never allowed fear to cause her to shy away from opportunities. She is active in our local church activities and my international ministry.

Lyric was approached about entering the world of pageantry, and my first thoughts immediately went to the images I had seen of little girls who looked beyond their age, covered in makeup, enlarged wigs, heels, fancy dresses, and lots of money. I remembered the death of a former young titleholder who was murdered, and the tabloids smeared her in magazines, stating how much makeup she wore at such a young age. The thoughts of our granddaughter with an extreme amount of makeup were not an option. To our surprise, this pageant system was focused on self-confidence and natural beauty, and makeup was forbidden in Lyric's age group. Gorgeous gowns were encouraged; however, the outward appearance was not the focus, so we accepted the invitation.

Lyric became the state beauty queen in her category and went on to compete in the national competition representing our state. She did not win the national competition. However, she placed high, had an awesome experience, and met amazing friends. Her experience as a contender for the crown was great because they focused on bringing out her inward beauty, personality, and talents.

Our family enjoyed watching her natural grace and beauty shine as she confidently took the microphone to introduce herself to the audience and walked the stage with class and elegance. Her dimpled smile could be seen in the back of the room. Her kinky hair was rolled into a bun that sat high upon her head; the pimple on her forehead and her fuzzy eyebrows remained uncovered, and nothing overshadowed the beauty she exuded from within. She won several awards, including most photogenic without being photoshopped.

Lyric's pageant experience was much different from our real world. Unfortunately, images of public personas on social media are not authentic or deceptive, and the persuasive gestures of photos create distorted views of self-imaging. The quest to be perfect is a constant chase that can never be attained because it is a lie, and no one is perfect but the Father, who is in heaven.

The effects of Hollywood and movie stars upon women and girls are catastrophic. Billions are spent on body images that have been digitally photoshopped to make you think that their idea of beauty should be your ambition. The cosmetic industry is constantly enhancing its tactics to make you more beautiful than you already are. Nothing is wrong with wearing makeup; it is a choice, but it should be an enhancement, not a replacement. The makeup application is removable, but your natural beauty, both within and without, is permanent.

Digital imaging has been a wonderful tool that allows one to alter things wrong in a photograph. There is absolutely nothing wrong with using it in moderation. However, there is a saturation of false images, and people set a standard of beauty that you do not know. True beauty is being who God created you to be and loving yourself for who you are without shame or fear.

An abundance of negative relationships between Photoshop use and young women's self-esteem can be harmful because of idealized beauty content and enhanced photos. I believe these images of an unattainable beauty standard cause suffering to young female minds, which are already prone to negative thinking, worry, and self-esteem issues. Setting media limitations and unfollowing those who photoshop their images as a standard for beauty can promote emotional healing. Follow accounts that post positive messages about your body and your values.

Photoshopping alters or distorts reality and can be deceptive depending on how dramatically the photos are altered. Photoshopping an image should be an enhancement, not a distortion of true beauty. Drastically altering who a person is can represent those preoccupied with outward appearance and low self-esteem. Changing who you are promotes many dangers of vanity, such as sinning against God, hurting others, and hurting yourself. James 4:6 says, "God opposes the proud but favors the humble." He wants us to be humble, compassionate, and kind. Vanity will not cause us to have any of these traits. The notion is that vanity is a sense of being preoccupied with outward appearance instead of inner beauty.

God defines beauty as a person who reflects His character. He does not want us to become preoccupied with the outside. Scripture reminds us that the Lord looks at people's hearts, not their outward appearance (1 Samuel 16:7). Thus, true beauty comes from the inside. Unlike the world, which tells us that people are attractive or lovely because of their appearance, the Bible tells us that beauty is based on character.

According to 1 Peter 3:3-4, "Your beauty should not come from outward adornments, such as braided hair and gold jewelry and fine clothes. Instead, it should be that of your inner self, the unfading beauty of a gentle and quiet spirit, which is of great worth in God's sight." In other words, when beauty comes as much from within as without, it magnifies their outer beauty. If you care for the inside, the outside will care for itself. There's nothing more beautiful than a person who exudes self-confidence and self-love.

You can exude inner beauty by focusing on inner qualities. Remember that true beauty goes beyond physical appearance. Cultivate qualities such as kindness, compassion, empathy, and confidence. Practice kindness towards yourself and others and let your inner beauty shine through in your interactions and relationships.

Inner beauty is important because it helps you appreciate outer beauty. Feeling good about yourself will make you feel more confident about facing and interacting with others. It comes from lovely thoughts; it evolves when you are happy for yourself and others; it is born from a place of self-acceptance, selflessness, and compassion. Your inner beauty shines when you are your authentic self and not photoshopped.

Father, I am who you say I am. I accept the full work of Calvary, and I boldly walk in purpose and the fullness of who I am unapologetically.

THE MEAN GIRL SYNDROME

The competitive environment among women is sometimes referred to as the mean-girl syndrome, often a disguise for fear or low self-esteem. Girls or women exhibiting offensive and overpowering behaviors may project a standoffish attitude that does not match what is happening inside. Jeremiah 17:9-10 emphasizes the importance of searching the heart and testing the mind.

"Mean Girl Syndrome" is when some girls act all mean. They do things to be popular or in control, even if it means being not-so-nice to others. It's like spreading rumors, talking behind someone's back, or making them feel left out.

It is not an official diagnosis or anything—it's just a way people talk about how some girls can be mean to each other, especially during high school. Dealing with this means promoting better communication, teaching empathy, and helping people learn how to handle conflicts without being all mean. Schools often have anti-bullying programs to create a friendlier atmosphere, and it's cool when parents and teachers talk to teens about this stuff to ensure everyone's being treated with respect.

Being a mean girl can find its roots in toxic, competitive environments that foster jealousy among women. Some believe that women struggle to get along because they view each other as rivals, often coveting the blessings God has bestowed upon others while underestimating what He has given them. Your presence or the evidence of God's blessings in your life may be seen as intimidating to some, but it's not your fault. Never dim your light to make others comfortable with what God is doing in your life. Instead, let God shine through you as a beautiful reflection of His glory because you are made in His image.

Engaging in competition with your sister is not friendly, especially when unaware of the hurdles she had to overcome to reach her current position. This aligns with the wisdom in Song of Solomon 8:6, emphasizing the need to set love as a seal on our hearts and arms. Love is powerful, while jealousy is as harsh as the grave, fueled by fiery coals. The root cause of jealousy lies in the inability to appreciate the blessings God has provided and a lack of gratitude. As James 3:16 warns, where envy and self-seeking exist, confusion and every evil thing follow. You don't have to measure up to someone else; be comfortable in your skin, regardless of its pigmentation.

A person with healthy self-esteem believes that they, as individuals, have a lot to offer – even if they may not be able to measure up to others in a competition. Essentially, they do not base their value on comparisons but on their value as humans.

Girls appearing angry, mean, and competitive might be using their attitudes to deflect attention from their low self-esteem, brokenness, fears, hurt, and rejection—a cry for love and acceptance despite their tough exterior. They are like turtles carrying hard shells for protection; prying opens their hearts and reveals their great value, much like opening an oyster to find precious pearls. Top of FormBottom of Form

Some girls with mean personalities have such low self-esteem because they house anger for one reason or another. Anger is one of the ten basic God-given emotions. Its impact can be either constructive or destructive, depending on how you respond. The key is to ensure that your emotions remain under control, aligning with God's design for our lives and prompting healthy changes in how we relate to others and fulfill our responsibilities. When we think of an angry person, the image that often comes to mind is someone no one wants to be around – someone slamming doors, yelling loudly, and making life miserable for everyone, including themselves. If anger is not handled properly, it can alter your behavior, and attitude, and eventually erupt from deep within your heart.

The first step toward freedom is recognizing and accepting responsibility for toxic patterns or behavior, especially in the realm of anger. Such behavior is detrimental not only to others but also to the individual harboring the anger. While we all have a profound need to express our hurts, frustrations, and anger, it is crucial to do so in a manner that avoids causing harm to others. The guidance from the Bible encourages us to experience anger without succumbing to sinful actions (Ephesians 4:26).

As you navigate the path toward recovery from any behavior not pleasing to the Lord, having Jesus Christ as your strength and guide will empower you to overcome the spirit of anger and low self-esteem.

Father, the things in my personality, generational curses, habits, and unkind ways that are not pleasing to you, please help me change into the image of Christ.

Black Sheep

A black sheep is created when there are two different changes in DNA or genes inherited from both the ewe (female sheep), and the ram (male sheep) to get black color (so-called recessive inheritance). If a white ram and a white ewe have traits for black, about one in four of their lambs will be black. In most white sheep breeds, only a few white sheep have traits for black, so black lambs are rare and unique. Lambs born with black wool could not be dyed any other color, so sheep farmers could not sell the wool, and black sheep were considered worthless.

The black sheep has been considered worthless in society, symbolizing rebelliousness and bad luck for centuries. In many cultures, the black sheep is an outcast, often used as a metaphor for someone who does not fit in with the rest of society. The more the black sheep are ridiculed, the less likely they are to make friends, open their hearts, and share things about themselves for fear of being rejected or not liked by their peers. The less they share, the more of an outcast they become.

Feelings of being a black sheep are created as a child and normally carry over into adulthood if you do not get healed emotionally from the damage caused by words, actions, or others. The black sheep in a family is marginalized, treated differently, or excluded by the rest of the family. When family members single out a black sheep, it shows that the family is not interested in understanding what God created differently, and they may not know how to include the black sheep. Shaming, name-calling, and ideas of perfection are created by the family, society, and the media, and false images such as size, color, status, or personality traits are highlighted.

The family's black sheep are the outcasts, seen as different and written off as weird, and they feel they do not fit into the family. On top of being considered weird, black sheep are often scapegoated and blamed for most of a family's problems. Sometimes, they are playfully teased; at worst, they are rejected because of the inability of others to accept anyone different from them. When your family does not see or value who you are, it is very difficult to see or value your true self.

Common signs of the family's black sheep include feeling like you don't belong, being excluded at events, or being isolated from your friends. Due to their uniqueness, many black sheep feel lonely, abandoned, isolated, or like an orphan. You hide your true self and don't allow yourself to do what you want right for you for fear of disapproval.

When a person experience stress or isolation, they show signs of depression by hanging their heads and avoiding connection with others. They may act out in ways to show their hurt and feelings. Sometimes, it is shown through anger, which can be misunderstood or considered a "mean girl" because they will not allow anyone to get close to them for fear of being hurt.

The Black Sheep is unconventional and disposed towards taking a different path than their family members. They are there to bring new ideas and spark change in the family, introducing them to something new. Even the negative habits of certain black sheep can lead to growth and healing for the family, so being a black sheep has benefits if you allow your uniqueness to shine bright.

Black sheep can explore what they want for their lives without worrying about what their family will think (since they will disapprove no matter what). The experience of being a black sheep also gives you a stronger sense of self, a greater ability to empathize with others, and the chance to discover yourself and others who are accepting of your uniqueness.

They can offer great wisdom in the world because they have a unique perspective. But for the world to benefit from their gifts, the black sheep must learn the spiritual lessons to be ready to connect and share. It is important to remember that being the black sheep of your family may not have anything to do with you and your behaviors. Being the black sheep does not mean anything is wrong with you. Some of the most common reasons people feel like the black sheep of their family include differences in overall values.

If you are the black sheep in your family and become successful, it can challenge and transform your family dynamics and narratives. Your achievements might inspire others, but they can also incite jealousy or attempts to undermine you. It is essential to distance yourself from toxicity.

Just as the black sheep is unique, so are you. You are so unique that no one has your exact features or DNA. Twins resemble each other, but neither is exact because God never made two people alike. Your uniqueness is what makes you special to God and the world. God was mindful of who you were before your birth. In Jeremiah 1:5, God says, "Before I formed you the womb, I knew you.

To be created in God's image means we have been given a unique status and divine dignity. It means that God has set you apart and made you a very special creation in this world. As Christians, you cannot forget the significance of this special honor that God has given you. Your life reflects the Lord when you shine light into the darkness by accepting yourself for who you are.

If you are the black sheep, you do not need to get others to accept you because God has already accepted you. That can give you so much freedom without having to please anyone.

How to embrace being a "black sheep"

1. The more you accept yourself and your differences, the more fun you will have as the black sheep.

2. Forgive yourself and others. ...

3. Do not internalize other's feelings about you because we are all flawed.

4. Keep your vibe high.

5. Find your tribe and hang out with other Black Sheep.

Father, I refuse labels, stigmas, and seeds of rejection attached to my life. I am no longer rejected but accepted into the family of God as your chosen vessel.

THE LOWDOWN ON GETTING REJECTED

Hey there, peeps! Let's dive into the rollercoaster ride of rejection, a topic we've all got a backstage pass to, whether we like it or not. Rejection, that unexpected plot twist in our lives, isn't just about slamming doors in our faces – it's more like a GPS redirecting us to cooler destinations. So, let's chat about why rejection isn't the end of the world but the start of something pretty darn awesome.

Rejection can contribute to the ugliness of low self-esteem, or it can be the catalyst to get you to reach your goals. It sucks if you allow it to cripple your progress. The truth is, everyone wants to be loved, valued, appreciated, and accepted regardless of your age, right? Unfortunately, everyone will not like you, just as everyone did not like Jesus. He was awesome, but most rejected Him and did not receive His message.

Feeling the Feels: Okay, so rejection hits you right in the feels – disappointment, sadness, maybe a dash of "What's wrong with me?" But guess what? It's cool to feel those things. Let those emotions flow, blast your favorite tunes, and remember, it's just a moment, not your whole story.

Failures are the Real MVPs: Picture this: failures are your VIP pass to the success party. Seriously! They're like the secret sauce that makes the victory taste even sweeter. Loads of big shots in history got rejection slapped on their faces before hitting the big leagues. So, embrace the failures, learn the lessons, and prepare for a comeback that'll blow everyone's minds.

Release the Superhero in You: Resilience is your superhero cape. It's what makes you bounce back from rejection stronger than ever. Think positive vibes, turning challenges into power moves, and always keep your eyes on the prize. Resilience is the weapon that turns setbacks into setups for greatness.

Rejection is a Detour, not a Dead End: When life throws a rejection curveball your way, it's not saying, "Game over." Nope, it's more like, "Hey, check out this detour – it might be the scenic route to your dreams!" Job rejection? Maybe that's the universe pushing you toward a cooler career. Breakup blues? Get ready for some solo self-love and epic adventures.

Empathy Rocks: Going through rejection amps up your empathy game. You get what it's like to hit a bump in the road, making you a total empathy rockstar. It's like having a backstage pass to connect with others on a deeper level. Shared vulnerability? That's the secret sauce to stronger connections.

Persistence is your Ride-or-Die buddy on this wild rejection journey. It's that inner voice saying, "I got this," when everything feels like a mess. Keep hustling, stay true to your goals, and show rejection that you're not just a player – you're the game-changer.

In a world of plot twists and unexpected turns, rejection is just one chapter of your story. So, don't sweat the small stuff, rock those resilient vibes, and prepare for the epic journey from rejection to your version of success. You've got this, and the world better be ready for the awesomeness you're about to unleash!

Father, I no longer see rejection as my life story. I release those who do not understand my value. I am beloved of God, blessed, and highly favored. You accept me as the apple of your eye.

BROKE PEARLS

Beneath the wild waves of the ocean floor hides one of Earth's most precious treasures—the pearl. She withstands the hustle and bustle of vacationers, mischievous pirates, and bustling boats, silently waiting for those who recognize her value. Though hidden for ages, those who uncover her zealously guard her, understanding her worth. Even when discovered in shattered and bruised states, pearls are kept safe until they can be worn again.

The tale of pearls and their creation is captivating; emerging from a dark, tumultuous place, they form from the agitation of sand captured by an oyster. You might feel like that oyster, facing life's challenges, but remember, it's how you're made.

Each pearl is unique, bought individually by jewelers for their distinct sizes and shapes. You're just like those pearls, one of a kind and essential. Your value increases with every challenge you endure. A skilled jeweler sees beyond outward appearances, creating masterpieces despite imperfections.

Preparing for a tea party, I struggled to find the perfect finishing touch one summer day. A string of pearls from my jewelry box added charm and elegance, turning my outfit into a conversation piece.

Little did I know, the pearls were hung on to another jewelry set; unfortunately, they broke and scattered all over the floor. I stood for a while in dismay. Even when they broke, I knew their value. Instead of discarding them, I used them to decorate a mirror, trash bin, and picture frame, transforming them into astonishingly beautiful pieces for our formal living room.

Walking into our formal living room and seeing what has become of the pearls is astonishingly beautiful. No one could ever imagine it was not the original intent. They are a conversation piece each time a person visits our home.

The pearls had been broken and shattered, but they were still usable. Some things have caused brokenness in your life, but God will still get glory out of every experience. You have value, and you are worthy.

Life may break you, but you're still usable like those pearls. God will bring glory out of your brokenness. Understand your worth, rooted in Him. Life happens to everyone, but it molds us into Christ's image, increasing our value.

In brokenness, you discover your worth and strengthen your relationship with God. Being broken allows you to see His power to heal and restore. Your broken parts will be used for God's glory, as Romans 8:28 assures us. God doesn't leave us broken; He heals the brokenhearted and binds our wounds (Psalm 147:3).

Embrace your brokenness, letting it make you better, not bitter. The vicissitudes of life don't diminish your value or worth. Hold your head high, for you've survived every broken piece. Rejoice in what adds value—faith, love, peace, health, strength, joy, and happiness.

Father, I pray that your healing power will make me whole and complete for every broken area. Take my brokenness and form it into a masterpiece for your glory.

FAILURE IS NOT AN OPTION

Failure is inevitable. This is a fact of life. However, how you perceive failure determines what path you take. The truth is, failure is not a permanent state of being it is not the end of the world, nor will it destroy your life unless you decide for it to. world-ending. Failure means you tried and didn't succeed, at least not during this round.

Your failures do not have to be fatal because God's grace is sufficient to help you recover. So, in the face of failure, what should you do? Try again, and never give up. The only true failure happens when we give up. Always keep your vision before you because it will come to pass if you remain steadfast and unmovable.

No one always wins because God does not want us to become prideful. Sometimes, we do not achieve our goals because it is our fault. We set the goal, and our actions did not achieve it; we must accept this truth. It can indicate that your goals may not align with who God wants you to be, or you may need to change something to make it work.

God uses failures to teach us valuable lessons about Him and ourselves. Either way, there is a learning opportunity to be had that will propel your life forward and enhance it in multiple ways. Always find the lesson in it. You can also pay it forward by teaching others what you learned.

The problem is that it's easy to beat ourselves up about it and resign this failure as a clear indicator of who we are. But this is not true. Ariana Huffington has said, "Failure is not the opposite of success. It is part of success."

Not to minimize it, but failure happens to the best of us. One does not get through life without a few serious slip-ups. This is what being human is all about.

The sooner you move past the denial stage, the better it is for you. Accept responsibility for it. And most importantly, understand that this does not define you. How you handle that slip-up shows your true characteristics, and you should take this information and run with it; let it empower, elevate, and cause you to excel!

Reflect on the failure and how to improve, but do not focus on it. Find out what went well and let that be your focus. Suppose this is a goal you want to continue with and plan to tackle the issues you faced during this round. If it's not a goal you want, ask yourself what you envision your future life to look like, then create goals around that.

Do not blame yourself or judge too harshly, as this will cause low self-esteem. Get up, dust yourself off, and keep moving because failure is not an option. \

Father, help me accept responsibility for my actions without shame or blame. Give me the courage to admit my contribution to why I failed this go-round and help me keep my eyes on you and my goals.

GAME CHANGER

You should not be surprised at anything that the devil is doing in your life because you are not wrestling against flesh and blood but against principalities, powers, and spiritual wickedness in high places.

The enemy's goal is to stop you before you realize who you are. He plays with your mind to discourage you in the discovery and to frustrate God's plan in your life. He wants you to give up before God's promises manifest in your life! Jesus said in Luke 22:31, "Satan has desired to have you, that he may sift you as wheat: But I have prayed for you, that your faith does not fail.

Satan has used shame, embarrassment, and labels to stop you. You are not your present and you are not your past. You are not poor, you are not left out, and you are not forgotten.

The enemy has thrown everything but the kitchen sink at you; he has sent his best generals to alter your view of the power you have within, and he is only doing it because you are a game changer, and you will always be victorious. II Corinthians 2:14 says now, thanks be to God, which always causes us to triumph in Christ and to make manifest the Savior of His knowledge by us in every place. In other words, the victory is won. The fight is fixed, and no weapon formed against you shall prosper.

You must understand who you are and actively pursue what God promised. Some folk wait for things to happen, others hope it happen, but when you understand who you are, you make it happen. You do not need to talk about it, be about it. Although God made promises to you, you must stand firm on them and begin to walk in authority by transforming your mind. Changing your mindset will create your movement, and your movement will create a new life.

Embrace a winner's attitude and begin to walk in victory. Winning takes grit and grace, which it takes to overcome any challenge. If you do not know how wonderfully made you are, you will never become all that God intended for you to be. You must remain resilient and tenacious and keep the faith amid great adversity.

Here are examples in the bible of men and a woman who were resilient.

1) David was a warrior and the first leader to fight and defeat the Amorites fiercely because he was unwilling to give up. He knew what abilities he had, and he knew God.
2) Bartimaeus was a blind beggar who beg for alms by the roadside daily. He heard Jesus was passing through the town, and he aggressively pursued his healing from Him while the crowd discouraged him from doing so. Because he refused to give up, Jesus stopped and healed him.
3) The woman with the issue of blood would not have gotten healed had she not fought through the crowd to touch Jesus' garment despite the law that declared her unclean.

Once you know who you are, the game is over! You are unstoppable if you realize that the same power that rose Jesus from the dead also lives within you. When you know who you are, who can stop you?

You are a real change-maker, representing a real threat to the world of darkness. You were born to conquer; you are called to tread upon serpents, cast out the devil, and win! In any situation God drops you in, you come out better. Like Joseph, you are gifted in a pit or a palace; you are gifted to take a seed and produce a harvest. I believe you are in a season of manifestation.

How you show up for yourself speaks to your confidence in God and you. Believing you can achieve whatever you put your mind to is not arrogant. You must always show up for yourself and let God shine within you. Square your shoulder, hold your head up, and let the devil know that he should have stopped you before you discovered how you were made fearfully and wonderfully.

I want to share a beautiful story from Numbers 26: the men had all died in the Wilderness. There had been a 38-year lapse since the first great census, and every Israelite man and woman over 20 years old except Caleb, Joshua, and Moses had died. Up to this point, the Hebrew law gave only sons the right to inherit their father's blessings. No laws allowed women to become recipients of the promise unless she was connected to a man. No provisions were made for them to receive the inheritance because of their gender. The odds were against them, but are not you glad that Jesus came? He came to set the captive free, and whatever is established in heaven is also established on the earth.

The father's name was Zelophehad, which means the shadow of fear. Satan wants to keep you walking in fear and under this shadow or the illusion of fear. Fear can cripple you from doing anything God wants you to do. He has not given you the spirit of fear but of power, love, and of a sound mind.

Fear will make you believe that it is too late. But where there is life, there is hope, and it is never too late for God's promises to manifest in your life. Many of you will not move in the things of God because you fear man, rejection, failure, opinions, being different, and some low self-esteem. Start making yourself a priority and believing in yourself.

The Bible says that Zelophehad had no sons, but he had five girls named Mahlah, Noah, Hoglah, Milcah, and Tirzah.

Each of Zelophehad's daughter' unique names gave us insight into their personalities. We must be careful that names and labels do not keep us bound to our situations.

Mahlah - Weak

You are stronger than you think you are because when you are weak, God is strong. The weaker the vessel, the stronger God's power is in your life. II Corinthians 12:9 says, my grace is sufficient for you, and my strength is perfect in your weakness.

Noah - Rest/walk in peace.

Life can be stressful if you do not find peace. Peace is a part of your inheritance. When things go crazy, you must put those things in God's hands. He will give me perfect peace if you keep my mind on Him.

Hoglah - Boxer/Fighter

There are times when you need to rest, but there are times when you must fight for what belongs to you. The key attribute of a fighter is they are resilient, and you must be also.

Milcah - Queen

A queen inherits the position by right of birth. You are born into the family of God, and you are royalty. Yes, your crown may be crooked, and you have flaws, but that does not change your God-given position. The Bible says you are a chosen generation, a royal priesthood, a holy nation, a peculiar people (I Peter 2:9).

Tirzah – Delight/Pleasant

Tirzah may be pleasing to the ear, but the feminine Hebrew name best suits those unafraid to abandon pleasantries and defy expectations. You must not settle and be willing to stand against injustice.

The five daughters of Zelophehad were women who were game changers. They refused to govern according to the laws of man and settled for less because their father had no sons, and they were treated poorly because they were girls. They changed the game when they realized what belonged to them and took risks that could have cost their lives.

What I saw was valuable is they all got together. They did not leave each other behind. Who else can benefit from what you know? No one can do anything in life alone. We were all made for each other. Unity is our superpower, and we are always better together.

They stood before Moses and Eleazar, the priest, and the priest and all the congregation, by the door of the Tabernacle of the congregation. The door represents access, transition, and opportunity. I believe your promise is at the door.

The daughters of Zelophehad challenged Moses by saying, "Our father died in the wilderness, and why should the name of our father be done away with because he had no sons? We know who we are, so give us what belongs to us.

The Bible says Moses prayed. The Lord said to him, "The daughters of Zelophehad have spoken right. Give them their father's inheritance.

God commanded Moses to change the laws on their behalf and future generations. The new law was, "If a man dies and has no sons, then you will cause his inheritance to pass to his daughters.

Just as the daughters of Zelophehad were game changers, so are you because you are chosen, gifted, anointed, and unique.

Father, thank you for choosing me to impact the world for myself and the generations coming behind me. I will not walk in fear, but I will be strong and courageous.

CONFIDENCE BOOSTER

The vote of confidence from others is rewarding, but what good is it for others to believe in you when you do not believe in yourself? The lack of confidence is fear, an unpleasant emotion caused by the belief that someone or something is dangerous and likely to cause pain or a threat. Fear can be crippling, and it can become a handicap. Living your life in fear with regret can create depression and anxiety, and it tears down your self-esteem. Fear is the lack of confidence in God and yourself. Fear anticipates failure, whether that is reality or not; it becomes truth to the person experiencing it. Acting confident can be exhausting because it is not authentic. Whether you are afraid or not, you must step out of your comfort zone and trust God with the outcome.

Confidence is speaking up for yourself and walking in your truth with boldness. God will give you the boldness to build your confidence and create opportunities to let your brilliance shine. You build your confidence by building your inner strength and personality and loving yourself as you are. Acting confident can be exhausting because it is not authentic, it is fake. Whether you are afraid or not, you must step out of your comfort zone and trust God with the outcome.

Many things are confident blockers:

Comparison. Stop comparing yourself to others because everyone's journey is different. You will never be in the same place as someone else, so stop judging your journey against someone else's journey.

Self-hate can kill your confidence. You cannot change your life with a wave of a magic wand, but you can take small steps toward doing the one thing that can transform your life.

Doubt is a confident killer. It is the love child of fear and anxiety. When you constantly second-guess your every move. You will never get to your destination or reach your goal. When you doubt, normally, you become a procrastinator and delay walking into your greatness.

Confidence is like having a strong belief in yourself and your abilities. Surely, you've got the skills and smarts to tackle whatever comes your way. When you're confident, you've got this positive vibe about who you are, recognizing what you're good at and being cool with the stuff you're still figuring out.

It is not just about thinking you're perfect or always having all the answers. It's more about knowing your strengths, accepting your weaknesses without feeling down about yourself, and just feeling good in your skin.

Confidence also means looking at challenges with a glass-half-full kind of attitude. Confident people tend to focus on the good stuff that could happen instead of stressing about things going wrong.

Being confident doesn't mean you're loud or pushy. It's about speaking up for yourself in a way that's cool and respectful to others. Confidence is walking in your truth with boldness. God will give you the boldness to build your confidence and create opportunities to let your brilliance shine. You build your confidence by building your inner strength and your personality and loving yourself the way that you are.

Many things are confident blockers, like comparison. Stop comparing yourself to others because everyone's journey is different. You will never be in the same place as someone else, so stop judging your journey against someone else's journey.

Self-hate can kill your confidence. You cannot change your life with a wave of a magic wand, but you can take small steps toward doing the one thing that can transform your life.

Doubt is a confident killer. It is the love child of fear and anxiety. When you constantly second-guess your every move. You will never get to your destination or reach your goal. When you doubt, normally, you become a procrastinator and delay walking into your greatness.

And when things get tough or you mess up, confidence helps you bounce back and learn from the experience. It's like seeing challenges as chances to grow, not as total disasters.

Taking risks is part of the confidence game, too. It's stepping out of your comfort zone because you trust yourself to handle whatever new stuff comes your way.

And hey, your body language is part of the confidence package. Standing tall, making eye contact, and just giving off positive vibes – that's the body language of someone feeling confident.

Remember, confidence isn't something you're just born with. It's like a muscle you can build up over time. It comes from doing things, learning, and realizing that it's okay not to be perfect. So, go out there, tackle challenges, and let your confidence shine!

Self-love, affirmations, pampering, and educational enrichment restore your confidence. Take a moment to give yourself a big hand and cheer yourself on as you step into unknown areas without fear. You will never know if you do not try.

So, what does God say about fear? The answer is simple: do not be afraid, for He is with us. May we rest in the words of Isaiah 41:10, "Fear not, for I am with you; be not dismayed, for I am your God; I will strengthen you, I will help you, I will uphold you with my righteous right hand, "God has not given you the spirit of fear but power, love, and a sound mind.

Father, I will not cast away my confidence; it will richly reward me. I will persevere so that when I have done the will of God, I will receive what you have promised.

17 WAYS TO OVERCOME LOW SELF-ESTEEM

1.   Talk to someone about how you feel.

Those who struggle with self-esteem issues should consult a mental health professional or someone that you trust. Raising low self-esteem is difficult to handle alone, particularly when it often arises from childhood trauma. Parents who give too much or too little praise can often cause self-esteem problems in their children. If they criticize you a lot as a child, you might turn to self-criticism. Looking at how your parents compared you to siblings or other children can often produce issues with self-esteem. Regardless of how it started, do not try to handle it alone or keep your feelings a secret. Satan wants you to keep silent about your feelings to keep you in bondage. Freedom begins when you share your thoughts with someone you trust.

2.   Learn from mistakes.

Remember that we are all human as you try to overcome your low self-esteem. I know this is easier said than done, but it is a must to overcome low self-esteem. Everyone, at some point in their life, will make a mistake. Try to understand that this is true, no matter how flawless they may seem. Learn to concentrate on your strengths, not your limitations. Do not overthink mistakes because you are human. You will keep making mistakes throughout your life, some more than others; all you need to do is learn from them.

One trick to overcoming low self-esteem is to learn not to beat yourself up when you make mistakes. Instead, learn from that mistake, pray about it, and use it to prevent you from repeating the same mistake in the future. Always remember that God's grace is extended to you.

3. **Release the past.**

Another way to overcome low self-esteem is to learn to live for now and not let the hurts of your past or worries about the future affect how you feel now. Let by gone be by gone, and let the present heal your past. Meditating on what happens to us causes internal damage to our self-worth. We have self-inflicted wombs when we have too many of these negative conversations.

You cannot redo what has already happened, but you can live in the present and change your future with the help of God. He is your refuge and strength and your present help. You made it through some tough times, but your future is bright. All these will draw you into the present and help you have the right frame of mind when making day-to-day decisions.

4. **Silence, critical inner voice.**

We all talk to ourselves, hopefully not out loud. What we say to ourselves is important. In beating low self-esteem, do not allow inner voices to command you. Stand up to them and overcome them by muting or reversing negativity. People with high self-esteem have learned to manage their critical thoughts, and they replace them with happy ones.

Women are multitaskers; our minds are busier, and we oftentimes worry too much about things we cannot change. Young women tend to worry constantly about what other people think about them, how they compare with peers, what's going to happen, and, of course, about their appearance. Indeed, starting in adolescence, women carry unhealthy emotions that can last for a lifetime if not dealt with. Add hormones to the mix, and things can go from bad to worse quickly. Young women, especially, have dramatic fluctuations in estrogen and progesterone each month, which can fuel negative thinking and worry even more. This can lead to low self-esteem and other emotional disorders, which affect health.

When negative thoughts enter your mind, you must think the opposite with something positive. Doing this initially will take some effort, but eventually, you will get better at thinking positively naturally. Unhelpful thinking makes you have feelings of depression, fear, anxiety, and sadness. If you lack confidence, it is only because there are thoughts in your mind that make you think, "Why am I not good enough?" Find out which thoughts are causing the low self-worth and work on changing them. No one can see the inside of your mind but you, so be truthful with yourself and realize you are not as bad as you think.

Constant negativity causes you to get "stuck" in negative thinking or negative behaviors and see the world as a cup half empty rather than half full, which can lead not just to low self-esteem but also to anxiety and depression.

So, instead of repeating negative thoughts, aim to stop them at the source. Every time a negative thought pops up, say, "Stop." Believe it or not, it does help quite a bit because it means you are now present rather than reliving the past or fearing the future. Remember that negative thoughts are just beliefs; they are not real. And before you even know it, you will have increased your confidence.

5. **Avoid toxic relationships.**

For the sake of your health, stop second-guessing yourself. It is wrong to do this to yourself. If you feel bad around toxic people, you shouldn't just take the abuse because you show signs of self-esteem problems. Instead, you should pray about cutting those people out of your life but not harbor unforgiveness because your main goal is to become spiritually and emotionally healthy. Deciding who should be in your circle is easier to improve confidence. The treatment for these issues will boil down to whether you listen to yourself.

6. **Recognize defense mechanisms.**

A defense mechanism is a subconscious reaction to a situation. Multiple defense mechanisms exist, such as projection, denial, repression, etc. If you feel guilty about something, you might use defense mechanisms to prevent yourself from internalizing your bad actions, thoughts, or life events. People with low self-esteem tend to use defense mechanisms without realizing it. It's possible that a build-up of too many negative events affected your self-esteem and caused you to protect yourself against more negative experiences. However, we all use defense mechanisms at one point or another. Make sure to recognize it when you find yourself doing it to avoid challenges in the future.

7.   **Avoid toxic relationships.**

What other people think about you can cause chaos to your self-esteem. Sometimes, the opinions of others can be constructive, and you could greatly benefit from them; however, not all opinions of you are good. It has been said that sticks and stones may break my bones, but words cannot harm me. Nothing can be further from the truth because words are powerful, and some words linger forever, depending on who said them. What we see and hear about ourselves significantly affects our self-esteem. And sometimes, those things may have a permanent effect.

Unfortunately, people do not talk about their flaws; they only talk about yours. So, you internalize it and believe their statement to be true. Believe it or not, the people you surround yourself with or interact with in the past have contributed to the person you are today. If you are trying to feel good about yourself, why surround yourself with people who hate themselves or have no life dreams, goals, or purpose? Spend time with positive people who want you to be better and who will push you to do the impossible.

We all want the same thing: to be accepted, loved, valued, and appreciated. We all want friends, but people who say bad things about you do not need to be in your space because they are toxic and bad for your mental health.

Find a person who celebrates you. The Bible says to have friends, you must be friendly. Stepping out of your comfort zone can create new friendships and bring people into your life who will celebrate you. The Bible says God is not mocked; whatever man sows, he shall reap. You should give away what you expect to receive.

8.   **Stop comparing yourself with others.**

To overcome low self-esteem, you must start learning to live your life and not try to please others. I know society has put expectations on you, but you don't have to meet all of them and never compare your achievements with those of others. Instead, set boundaries and goals and follow your dreams. God has a plan for your life; that is the course you should follow, not someone else's. Remember that we are all different, and each has something unique to deliver. Once you can learn to stop comparing yourself to others, you can be much happier with yourself.

9.   **Make personal improvements.**

Many things can lead to low self-esteem. Some are not in your control, while others are in your power to change. For example, if you're struggling with body dysmorphia, which is a mental health condition where a person spends a lot of time worrying about flaws in their appearance, it could hurt your self-esteem.

For instance, if you are overweight, you can start exercising, such as mindful walking and practicing mindful eating. When you exercise and eat right, your body will have numerous positive changes in how you feel and look.

If you are feeling tired all the time, which is one of the things that lowers your self-esteem, then you can overcome this by turning off the computer and television a few hours earlier and trying to get at least 8 hours of good sleep every night. This will help keep your mind and body healthy, give you more energy, and help you accomplish more throughout the day. Examine your life, highlight the areas where you can improve, work on those areas, and commit them to God in prayer.

10. **Try something new.**

One common characteristic of people suffering from low self-esteem is the feeling that they are incompetent or underperforming. They think that they are incapable of accomplishing certain things. Sadly, this is many times a self-fulfilling prophecy. To overcome low self-respect, you must understand that you can do more than you think and do all things through Christ, who gives you the strength to do so.

You can start by trying something new, like taking a class doing something you love. If your beliefs about yourself are true, and you fear you have low self-esteem because you are not good enough, develop new skills. Life will be better if you are constantly improving yourself.

You can also try something you have never done before. It does not matter what it is as long as you do something new because nothing beats a failure but an effort to try. You can read books, study, join support groups, or take classes in areas where you need improvement. You will learn and build your confidence with each new adventure or skill. With time, you will learn that there is nothing you cannot do when you believe in yourself. Most of all, get out of your way and remember that God can help you overcome every area in your life.

11. **Appreciate yourself and know where you shine.**

Self-appreciation and self-acceptance are two different things but are connected. You can't appreciate yourself if you do not accept yourself. One of the signs of low self-esteem is that you cannot see the good you have. Negative thinking can be the cause of why you cannot see all the good you possess.

You can build self-esteem by writing down all your good qualities. Examine your life, highlight the areas where you do better, work on those areas, and commit them to God in prayer. You can ask a friend or even your family members for help. Ask people for positive feedback to know what people value in you. You might write down a list of good habits you have, too. So, list at least ten helpful qualities you have, and overcome your negative beliefs about yourself.

Too often, we choose things we know we cannot accomplish and spend all our time and effort on them. Instead, know your niche and where you're good at, and then focus your hard work, persistence, dedication, and persistence on that. We all have areas where we do not excel, so stop criticizing when you fail at something. No one is perfect but Jesus.

12. **Self-care**

One of the things that contribute to low self-esteem is a constant feeling of stress and a tendency to abandon yourself. So, knowing how to take care of yourself is important, and this will lead to more low self-esteem.

Self-care is a biblical principle in Matthew 22:39: "Love your neighbor as you love yourself." Being kind to yourself creates self-love, and it helps you realize that you deserve it. Practice love and kindness to yourself just as you would a dear friend because you are your best friend. Sometimes, we may be kind to our friends and family but forget to extend that kindness to ourselves. Why would you be kind to others but be hard on yourself? One of the tricks for overcoming low self-esteem is treating yourself just like you would treat your best pal by caring, gentleness, and forgiveness. The most important person to you is you. It means cutting off the negative self-talk and encouraging yourself with positive affirmations that are believable to you.

Remember, it is not about how other people see you but how you see and treat yourself. The least you can do is be proud and celebrate yourself like a trusted friend. If you are angry at yourself, you can be proud of yourself. You are amazing, be proud of who you are. You are special.

Some days, loving yourself is easier said than done because all habits die hard. Think of a time when a close friend has felt bad about themselves or struggled somehow. Imagine what you say to them and how you want them to feel. Put yourself in that person's place and be your best friend.

Take time to do something you find relaxing or enjoyable. Try doing things such as taking a bath, gaming, meditation, singing, indoor dancing, stopping, listening to the melodious sounds of birds, feeling the breeze of air on your skin, smelling the freshness of the air, and enjoying the beautiful color of the sky. Take time to smell the coffee or roses around you. This will reduce your stress and help you feel better about yourself. You deserve it.

13. **Help others.**

The secret to having a healthy self-esteem is to boost it through showing kindness to others and good deeds. If you are struggling to see your positive qualities, all you need to do is help them shine. You will get a lot of positive feedback by helping people, cheering them on when they win, and being supportive overall. You will reap many rewards if you improve another person's life. And slowly but surely, your self-esteem will improve. You will have more self-compassion because you see the effort you put in. Keep planting seeds for others and not let life make you bitter but better.

14. **Be self-compassionate.**

Are your friends perfect? When they fall, you pick them back up. Give yourself the same permission to be imperfect, just like. Every other human being. Self-compassion is a balance. And you can cut yourself slack when you slip up or if things don't go your way. While still being accountable for your actions. You think kind, encouraging thoughts about yourself when things are fantastic and not going so well. Studies show that when you take your successes and failures in stride, you may be less afraid of failure and more satisfied with living your life. People who practice self-compassion are more likely to treat themselves well.

15. **Boost your body image.**

Improvements in your body are good if done with a proper motive and appreciation for who you are. We are all made and shaped differently; it is easy to blame your body for being too tall, too short, too squishy, too pale,

It's easy, but it is also unhealthy to think of yourself in such a harsh way. Remember, God skillfully and wonderfully made you. He is insulted when you do not appreciate His creation because He thinks it is good. You must embrace your body, celebrate its strengths, and honor what it has done and continues to do for you. Respect who you are and where you are on your journey. You can learn to appreciate and value your body even as you work to change it. Negativity about your body image can impact success in changing it. You must see yourself the way God sees you. you are made in the image of God, and everything that he made is beautiful; that includes you.

16.   Embrace happiness.

Happiness is a choice and not an event. You must choose to receive the joy of the Lord in your heart and live a happy life despite what is happening around you. God created this world for us to enjoy, so you must learn that life is not perfect. Choose to walk in the fruit of the Spirit and allow God to bring joy to your heart.

No one is promised the next moment, second, day, or hour. We must all learn to live and be mindful of our moment. Take advantage of your time on earth and maximize all God has given you. Being distracted and the things. This world can take you off course and cause you to become unappreciative of who and what you have.

17. Start to practice.

Living a mindful life. Be here Now is not just a New Age slogan. A growing body of evidence suggests that paying attention to the present without judgment can help you feel more optimistic. Higher self-esteem and happier relationships will enhance your life and help you succeed. Just breathe.

Finally, you must confront the hurts that held you captive; speaking about them, speaking to them, and speaking through them will help frame your thinking, feelings, and ultimately how you live your life. You are not your situation; it is a hurdle you will overcome. The experiences that you are having will be the lemon that makes a perfect glass of lemonade. You must become your best cheerleader and see yourself as God sees you. You must love yourself despite what you have done or what has been done to you because you are worth it.

You do not need to beat yourself up or feel incompetent whenever you mess up. Do not let humanness disrupt your learning experience. Let this book remind you to practice self-compassion. Accept yourself, love yourself, forgive your mistakes, commit your flaws to God, and feel your self-esteem soar.

Identify your thoughts; we all have thousands of thoughts a day. Some are helpful, but many are harmful, and they can undermine your success. Identify your thoughts and work to shift them to positivity.

Father, I am an overcomer. I accept myself, forgive my mistakes, correct my flaws, and continue to become all you want me to be.

YOU ARE STRONGER THAN YOU KNOW

Let's face it: life can be brutal sometimes, beating down and even breaking some of the strongest of us. Society can be hard and indifferent, always sending new challenges and obstacles our way. Sometimes, it feels like we never get a break from all the problems in life, with unexpected troubles hurtling towards us. Other times, it's just us with our weaknesses and flaws. Maybe we aren't cut out for that kind of challenge. Maybe we have grown weary over the years.

Here's the thing: no one is immune to mistakes, exhaustion, or failure...they are part of life. However, experiencing these things doesn't mean you are weak. It is a strong indication that you are resilient.

Taking responsibility for your actions shows you are stronger than you think. Taking This might seem like a petty quality, but it is not. It indicates that you believe that the quality of life you lead depends on what you mostly do. That acceptance alone gives you a sense of purpose and direction, a strength many lack. responsibility is a rare quality found in only the strong.

The truth is that not everyone likes or supports all that you do. We all need some degree of external validation to function in society. This means that relying on the approval of others puts you in a perpetual place of confusion and unhappiness, two potent poisons that take away your inner power. But people who limit that need to depend only on their important people (like family) will do better. You trust your competence and your ability to deliver. When the opportunity comes, you can be sure you will be ready. Your strength keeps you from relying on external validation; it comes from within.

Values are the last things that come to mind when discussing strength, yet they are huge internal strength indicators. Values take a lot of observation, experience, thinking, and deciding to form and require even more effort to stand by. You are strong if you can stand by your values in trying moments.

A lot of people give up on their dreams and aspirations. You are strong if you still have the fire in your eyes, the enthusiasm and determination to chase your dreams.

Mark Twain said that continuous improvement is better than delayed perfection. With the pursuit of a better life comes the grit and persistence needed to keep getting better. Strong people work on their skills and abilities. They practice, try, fail, and repeat till they succeed, and then they keep improving. You do not run away from work nor complain about problems when they arise, but rather tackle them head-on.

When emotions overwhelm, strong people take a step back to look at things objectively. They do not jump to conclusions or allow themselves to be influenced by their emotions – no matter how strong. They realize that emotions are fast and fleeting, but decisions last.

Being able to go up against what you fear is a strong indicator of courage and strength. Many people cannot talk to someone they like, make new friends, try something new, or ask their boss for a raise. Being able to face your fears is a huge indicator you are stronger than you think.

Strong people do not wear masks or foster jealousy. If you can cheer others on and celebrate their wins with them, you are confident in your affairs because you know your time will come. You do not pretend to be anyone but who you are. You are not attaching your self-worth to the things you have or what people say and think but to who you are. If you find yourself okay with being yourself, then you are strong.

Gratitude is a form of strength. Gratitude for friends, family, food, health, life, and all the tiniest of things in it. Thanking God for what He has done for you demonstrates enormous strength.

Numerous things are bigger than any one of us. If you can care about God's purpose for your life more than your desires, you are stronger than you give yourself credit for.

Even in the face of rejection, failure, abandonment, and despair, if you can find yourself at peace, know that without an ounce of doubt, you are stronger than you give yourself credit for.

Many people consider just being able to try again and to keep going an accomplishment, depending on what they are going through. Continuing to look for hope, solace, and a way out. You have made it through all the yesterdays of your life – and here you are, pushing towards tomorrow. After all, it's always hardest to give yourself a pat on the back, right? Indeed, you are stronger than you give yourself credit for. But sometimes, we all need a reminder of how far we have come.

RM Drake asked, "How could you think you are weak whenever you break? You come back stronger than before.

Christopher Robin, Winnie the Pooh, said, "You're braver than you believe, stronger than you seem, and smarter than you think.

You are stronger than you think. If any of these resonate with you, I hope they encourage you to appreciate who you are, what you do, and how much you are trying. You are stronger than you know.

Father, I can do all things through Christ, who strengthens me. Your strength provides me with the wherewithal to accomplish all I set my mind to do.

CREATE THE LIFE YOU WANT TO LIVE

What does it mean to create the kind of life you desire? It means you must put forth the effort and faith while cooperating with a God-given plan for your life. It has been said we are waiting on God, but the truth is God is waiting on us. He established a plan for your life before the foundation of the world. It is your assignment to find that plan and work it out.

I saw things on television that created false narratives when I was younger. I thought a prince would come on a white horse, sweep me off my feet, drive to a fabulous castle upon a steep hill, and we live happily ever after. This quickly changed when I woke up from my dreams and started to live. I found out the white horse, castle, and Prince Charming all came with efforts on my part. I had to create the life I wanted with the help of God.

Life is not perfect, as there is no such thing. It is not a straight line; it is full of bumps in the road. Life is a journey on a roller coaster that sometimes goes up, down, and all around. There will be many happy days and times when you can rejoice over what you have accomplished, but it did not get to this point without trials, pain, tribulations, tests, and tough lessons. It took a major effort on your part.

But we stand (or sit) here today and call in more peace, joy, positive experiences, unconditional love, and much more laughter.

I'm right there with you, believing in the best for you and your loved ones. Here are some helpful insights and tips to help you create the kind of life you want.

It all begins with connecting with God because He knows everything there is to know about you. He is where we find love and value. He is our ultimate love and true friend, and He came so you may live life abundantly. When your relationship with Him is correct, He will guide you into rediscovering yourself and help you create the life you want to live.

Creating the life you want to live means falling deeper in love with yourself. It is never the responsibility of others to love you; it is yours. Yes, being loved by others is wonderful, but solely relying on them for self-worth sets you up for disappointment. I spent far too long seeking security from other people. It oftentimes left me feeling disappointed and frustrated. If you're not happy with yourself, make some changes.

Take the necessary steps to reclaim who you truly are, a beautiful being with so much potential. Maybe it's time to excavate to see what's happening under the surface. There could be some negative emotions or old wounds that you need to attend to and heal. Maybe you've been through traumatic situations that made your brain gravitate toward the negative. Excavating takes work, but it's well worth it! Once you get to the core of yourself, you can straighten your crown and begin to live the life you deserve.

The easy thing to do is numb out, run, escape, or ignore it all. But that won't get you far in creating your desired life. You can make changes; start with a clean slate and nurture yourself lovingly as you navigate daily.

A few years back, I addressed an issue of my past that was buried for me to create the life I wanted to live. I opened old wounds so I could heal from depression, anxiety, anger, shame, fear, bitterness, disappointment, resentment, insecurity, codependency, and more to heal and discover the real me. The me that is pure, sweet, thoughtful, loving, giving, radiant, and free.

You must commit to change and the work it takes to create the life you want to live. Nothing changes if nothing changes. So often, we say we want to change, yet year after year, we're still the same.

Whether it's living in scarcity, fear, lack, depression, working a job we hate, etc., we show up at the end of the year scratching our heads, wondering why not much has changed.

The reality is that if you want to see change, you've got to make some changes by adopting a better, more positive mindset. The mindset you have today you can change. If it's good, you can make it better. If it's negative, you can make it more positive. Try not to limit yourself. Refuse to let negative thoughts control your life.

Life and death are in the power of your tongue; start telling a new story, the kind you want to live out! I can attest that your thoughts, beliefs, and words matter! Of course, it's not magical. You don't just think about something; it pops up out of nowhere, but what you focus your intent on matters.

If you continually beat yourself up with thoughts like, "I'm a failure" or "No one likes me", those thoughts become beliefs. And those beliefs tend to cause you to speak and act in certain ways that may cause you to fail at something or push people away.

But if you begin changing your mindset, your energy will change. Your vibes can go from negative to more positive. And rather than fail or push people away, you may find yourself achieving goals and making friends!

For years, I missed a lot of things because I was heavily in the church. Some of the teachings were in error because the elders wanted us to live a godly life, or perhaps their understanding was limited based on what they were taught. I spent a good bit of my life being too serious.

I remember thinking about how badly I wanted to be free to laugh, be goofy, and even dance! Growing up in an abusive, dysfunctional household where I had to walk on eggshells may have had something to do with this.

Eventually, I'd had enough of the serious life and decided to start having fun. I went from one activity that made me happy to another to another, and so on. I just started doing little things that made me feel happy. I started creating the kind of holidays I missed in my youth, throwing myself birthday parties, dancing, and listening to clean music. I bought things that I dreamed of having. It felt amazing to enjoy life. To loosen up and have fun – despite whatever is happening?

You can create the kind of year you have been dreaming of. Make time for fun, and commit to doing more things you enjoy, no matter your circumstances. Here's to creating the kind of life you desire, one step and one day at a time.

Father, you came that I may have life abundantly. Thank you for helping me live according to your word.

WOMEN OF THE BIBLE WITH CROOKED CROWNS

A woman adorned with a slightly askew crown exhibits fearlessness in the face of challenges, acknowledging her imperfections while allowing God to work through her for extraordinary purposes. Confident in their beliefs and unafraid to confront difficulties, these women inspire courage in others, urging them to make a positive impact despite their flaws and limitations.

While it's common to perceive biblical figures as flawless, the reality is that they were imperfect individuals chosen by God to showcase His glory through their lives. Women with crooked crowns draw strength from overcoming significant adversities or sins, emphasizing God's transformative power.

Numerous women in the Bible serve as inspiration, not just for their actions but for their unwavering faith amid challenging circumstances, all while wearing metaphorical crooked crowns.

Consider Mary, the mother of Jesus, who initially feared the angel's announcement but straightened her crown of fear to declare, "I am the Lord's servant. May it be to me as you have said" (Luke 1:38).

Hannah, a Levite woman, faced the crooked crown of barrenness but straightened it through fervent prayer, ultimately receiving the blessing of a son named Samuel.

Sarah, who laughed at God's promise due to her age and impatience, straightened her crown by demonstrating faith and obedience, trusting in God's promises despite her initial skepticism.

Once an idol worshipper, Ruth straightened her crown by turning away from her past and embracing the living God, becoming a pivotal figure in the lineage of King David.

Though dedicated and hardworking, Martha wore a crooked crown of misplaced priorities. Despite this, she utilized her day for productivity while learning the importance of balancing her work with spending time with the Lord.

Like us, these women embraced their crooked crowns, which had flaws, but their strength emanated from physical prowess and mental and emotional resilience. They overcame fears, insecurities, and identity struggles, rising above these challenges for a divine purpose rooted in something greater than outward beauty or personal accomplishments. Their stories exemplify the transformative power of faith and perseverance in the face of imperfection.

Father, there is no one perfect except you. Like the women you used in the bible as examples, I accept my flaws and pray by your grace I can overcome them all.

INSPIRATIONAL QUOTES

Life has many hurdles and tribulations, but don't let them get you down. You have complete control to change your feelings and your thoughts. Find strength in the inspiration from the following quotes and build your self-esteem. Like a cup of coffee, these short inspirational quotes can help you get your day started in the best way possible. Consider them a 'pick-me-up' when you don't feel your best.

"What you get by achieving your goals is not as important as what you become by achieving your goals." – Henry David Thoreau.

"I can't change the direction of the wind, but I can adjust my sails to always reach my destination." – Jimmy Dean.

"The best way to get started is to quit talking and begin doing." - Walt Disney.

"The only limit to our realization of tomorrow will be our doubts of today." – Franklin D. Roosevelt.

"You miss 100% of the shots you don't take." – Wayne Gretzky.

"Start where you are. Use what you have. Do what you can." – Arthur Ashe.

"Optimism is the one quality more associated with success and happiness than any other." – Brian Tracy.

"Whether you think you can or think you can't, you're right." – Henry Ford.

"Knowing is not enough; we must apply. Wishing is not enough; we must do." – Johann Wolfgang Von Goethe.

"Believe you can, and you're halfway there." – Theodore Roosevelt.

"Life is like riding a bicycle. To keep your balance, you must keep moving." – Albert Einstein.

"Nothing is impossible. The word itself says, "I'm possible!" – Audrey Hepburn.

"Life isn't about getting and having; it's about giving and being." – Kevin Kruse.

"Change your thoughts, and you change your world." – Norman Vincent Peale.

"Develop an 'attitude of gratitude.' Say thank you to everyone you meet for everything they do for you." – Brian Tracy.

"Success is not final; failure is not fatal: it is the courage to continue that count." – Winston Churchill.

"You do not find a happy life. You make it." – Camilla Eyring Kimball.

"It isn't where you came from; it's where you're going that counts." – Ella Fitzgerald.

"It's not whether you get knocked down, it's whether you get back up." – Vince Lombardi.

"I've missed more than 9000 shots in my career. I've lost almost 300 games. 26 times, I've been trusted to take the game-winning shot and missed. I've failed over and over and over again in my life. And that is why I succeed." – Michael Jordan.

"Every strike brings me closer to the next home run." – Babe Ruth.

"Life is 10% what happens to me and 90% of how I react to it." - Charles Swindoll.

"Challenges are what make life interesting and overcoming them is what makes life meaningful." – Joshua J. Marine.

"You are never too old to set another goal or to dream a new dream." – C.S. Lewis.

"Nothing in life is to be feared, it is only to be understood. Now is the time to understand more, so that we may fear less." – Marie Curie.

"Happiness is not by chance, but by choice." – Jim Rohn.

"Be the change that you wish to see in the world."- Mahatma Gandhi.

"If I cannot do great things, I can do small things in a great way." – Martin Luther King, Jr.

"We become what we think about." – Earl Nightingale.

"Remember no one can make you feel inferior without your consent." – Eleanor Roosevelt

"I may not have gone where I intended to go, but I think I have ended up where I needed to be." – Douglas Adams.

"Life isn't about finding yourself. Life is about creating yourself." – George Bernard Shaw.

"If you don't like the road you're walking, start paving another one." – Dolly Parton.

CROOKED CROWN AFFIRMATIONS

(You must perpetually speak life, affirmations and confess the word God).

I am loved, valued, appreciated and worthy.

I am beautiful, smart, and resilient.

God decided who He wanted me to be, and others do not have the power to change it.

God created me unique, and He did not duplicate the original.

I will not waste my life with regret, fears, people-pleasing, or limitations.

This is my year of self-discovery and self-awareness.

I am worthy, blessed, highly favored, and enough.

I let go of the need to figure everything out or to be perfect.

I release fear, depression, and anxiety from my life.

I fully accept myself for who I am because I am made in the image of Christ.

I am fearfully and wonderfully made.

I am being guided toward more joy and peace.

I appreciate what I have right now.

I am attracting the solutions that I need right now.

I am open to receiving new possibilities.

I will keep pushing toward my goals.

I always find the right approach to overcome obstacles.

I will believe in God and me.

I can do all things through Christ, who gives me strength.

No matter how much the enemy rages today, I will succeed.

I am destined for greatness.

I refuse depression, and I accept the joy of the Lord.

God will never let me down because He is my friend.

I can have what I believe.

Today is my day, and I will pick myself up and get going.

I will find the people who are assigned to help me reach my goal.

I will aim higher than I did yesterday.

This is my day of double, breakthrough, and breakout.

This is my day of healing, mental health, peace, happiness, and spiritual revival.

This is my day of strategic planning and fulfilling my purpose in God.

This is my day to draw closer to God, as I have never drawn close to him.

This is the day I will come out of fear and walk into spiritual authority.

This is my day to get a new plan and for God to stretch me.

This is my day to grow, thrive, and flourish.

This is my day for growth and increase.

God is preparing to promote and take me to places I have never imagined.

My family, marriage, friendships, and everything connected to me are blessed.

The blessings of the Lord will find me wherever I am.

I am the head and not the tail, above and not beneath.

I call forth a constant stream of blessings.

Everything that has been withheld from me will spring forth.

I am blessed in the city and blessed in the country.

The LORD will grant me prosperity, and the fruit of my womb is blessed.

The LORD will send a blessing on everything I put my hand to.

The LORD will open the heavens and send rain upon my dry ground.

I will lend to many nations but will borrow from none.

God will Remember Me like Naomi.

God will protect me like Hagaar.

God will heal me like the woman with the issue of blood.

God favors me like Ruth.

God prospers me like a virtuous woman.

God will use me like Mary Magdalene.

God answers me like Ruth.

God leads me like Deborah.

God intervenes for me like Esther.

WORKSHEET 1

Hopefully, this book has inspired you to discover how wonderful you are. With knowledge comes power, but that is effective only if you put it to work in your life. No one can unleash the power within you but you. You must begin immediately to do the hard work it takes to see the changes necessary to live a happy life and build your self-esteem. Are you willing to do the work? If so, read and complete each assignment.

Make a radical commitment to journeying toward them and do your best to enjoy the process. If you need help, don't be afraid to ask for it. There are plenty of people ready and willing to help.

The number five in the Bible is the number of graces. Healing from damaged emotions and understanding your worth requires you to extend grace to yourself. Use the exercises below to do so, and feel free to get an additional sheet of paper to complete your thoughts.

List five things you love about yourself. (It is okay if you do not have all five; work up to that number).

1._____

2._____

3._____

4._____

5._____

Describe yourself in five words:

1. _____

2. _____

3. _____

4. _____

5. _____

Please provide a list of your five least favorite attributes.

1. _____

2. _____

3. _____

4. _____

5. _____

What are your strengths?

_____
_____
_____
_____
_____
_____
_____

When asked to consider your self-worth, do you feel confused or may need a minute to answer? Why?

_____
_____
_____
_____
_____
_____

Would you say you have a high self-worth? _____.

Do you automatically start thinking about all the awesome things you love about yourself or immediately go to the negative when asked to consider how much you value yourself? _____.

Write something unpleasant, then add something positive beside it.

_____   _____

_____   _____

_____   _____

_____   _____

_____   _____

Think of a specific time when you have felt bad about yourself or struggled. What do you typically think or do? What do you say to yourself? Even your tone of voice matters.

_____

_____

_____

_____

_____

_____.

Is there a difference between the two answers? Why? Ask yourself why you would treat yourself any differently than you would treat a friend.

_____
_____
_____
_____
_____
_____.

Close your eyes and take a breath. Now, write down how you might respond to your struggles like you would respond to your friend.

_____
_____
_____
_____
_____
_____.

The next time you are feeling down or discouraged, try speaking to yourself in a more compassionate, understanding way and note how being more compassionate to yourself makes you feel.

After you truthfully answer all questions, list the changes you will make this coming year. Start small, be consistent and build up.

_____

_____

_____

_____

_____

_____

WORKSHEET 2

You can challenge yourself by truthfully asking the following questions. Feel free to get an additional sheet of paper to complete your thoughts.

1. Are the stressful or negative thoughts true? _____.

2. How do you react when you believe those thoughts?
   _____

3. Who would you be without the thought? Or how would you feel if I did not have the thought?
   _____
   _____

4. What dreams have you let go of, and how can you rediscover yourself?
   _____
   _____
   _____
   _____
   _____

5. What plans can you put in place to rebuild yourself spiritually and emotionally?

_____
_____
_____
_____
_____

6. What feelings of self-doubt would you like to release and change?

_____
_____
_____
_____
_____

7. How can you create a new circle of friends and support?

_____
_____
_____
_____
_____

8. What are your plans for trying something new?

_____
_____
_____
_____

9. What are your self-improvement goals?

_____
_____
_____
_____

Commit to affirming yourself in a fun, loving way daily. Those days you feel bad, extend grace and continue another day, but do not revert to old habits. Remember, practice makes perfect.

Epilogue

Okay, so picture this epic journey, right? It's like the ultimate quest for feeling awesome about yourself. Our main character, let's call her "You," starts on this wild ride full of self-discovery and battling those mega-doubts and haters inside and out.

So, here's the deal: picture your crown, right? It's not all neat and symmetrical; it's got some crazy twists and turns, maybe a little crooked. And guess what? That's what makes it perfect. Your quirks, flaws, and unique vibes are like the jewels on your crown.

Along the way, you face all these crazy challenges that try to mess with your self-worth, society's expectations, inner demons, and the whole drama. But guess what? You will straighten your crooked crown, rise to the occasion, grow stronger and more resilient, and embrace your true self because you are fierce and wonderfully made.

Fast forward, you are not a flawless superhero. Nah, you've got battle scars, but you wore them like badges of honor. Each scar tells a story of overcoming tough stuff and embracing imperfections. Self-acceptance became your superpower, grounding them in knowing that you deserve love, success, and all the good stuff.

But, hey, this story isn't one of those "happily ever after" deals. It's more like an ongoing saga. The journey never really ends because self-esteem is a forever thing. You must keep looking within, showing yourself some love, and growing.

And it's not just about You. This tale has a ripple effect on the whole squad—friends, family, the whole crew. As You rock that self-love vibe, it spreads. Communities strengthen, diversity is celebrated, and the comparison game is shut down.

Now that you are aware of the tactics used to hold you captive choose to live in freedom. You can learn to tame your busy brain by meditating on the word of God or thinking of beautiful things or things that make you happy. You can counter some of these confidence-killers and use them to straighten your crown.

The epilogue isn't some final chapter. It's a high-five to the human spirit's power to bounce back from doubt and reach new heights of self-love. It's an invitation for everyone to join the adventure, dig into their own stories, and realize that the journey to feeling awesome is like a forever thing, full of crazy twists, life lessons, and moments of pure awesomeness.

Every knock, bruise, or painful experience makes your crown shine. They all make you the beautiful person you are, so remove the unnecessary perfection pressure because it does not exist. Wearing your crown, a little crooked, and knowing that the journey to perfect self-esteem is about embracing the beautifully imperfect YOU. Keep shining, you amazing human! Square your shoulders, hold your head high, twirl, and embrace your **CROOKED CROWN** because it is perfect!

MEET THE AUTHOR

Dr. Tanda Canion is an innovative, creative thinker, writer, author, entrepreneur mentor, and God's mouthpiece preaching and bringing deliverance to the Body of Christ. As God's anointed vessel, Dr. Canion has embraced the mission to preach the Gospel of Jesus Christ without compromise to the nation and the world.

Dr. Canion attended the following universities: Clark Atlanta University, Georgia State University, and Beulah Heights University. Dr. Canion earned a doctorate in theology at Kingdom First Christian University and received Honorary Doctorate degrees from the Anointed by God Ministerial Seminary and Kingdom First Christian University. She is a Life Insurance Agent, Notary Public, and a former Real Estate Agent licensed in Georgia. She is also a certified interior designer from Clayton State University.

With over several decades of ministry, Dr. Canion is a seasoned Elder and Evangelist known for her transparency and candid delivery of God's Word. Because of her willingness to serve and to conduct ministry with passion and excellence, God has expanded her ministry in the following areas:

- Bible Teacher
- Convention/Conference Speaker and Host

- Seminar Speaker

- Guest on multiple media platforms, including TBN, The Word Network, and more.

Dr. Canion is the visionary and founder of Tanda Canion Ministries, Tanda Canion Foundation, and the Tanda Canion Empowerment Conference. Through her obedience to God, lives are being changed, chains are broken, and people from all walks of life are being empowered with tools daily. Outside of the pulpit, Dr. Canion is a community activist and leader. As an activist, Dr. Canion has prayed and marched on the State Capitol for State House-Led Bill 816 to put prayer back into school.

Dr. Canion has actively partnered with AARP and the Susan G. Komen Foundation and is using her voice to bring awareness to breast cancer and women's health. Through this partnership, she has hosted panel discussions on the deadly disease with Atlanta's top physicians and surgeons.

Dr. Canion advocates adult and teen literacy in the community with the Assembly of Truth Family Worship Center to provide weekly classes. She is the founder and CEO of the Tanda Canion Foundation, which hosts Back to School drives and gives youth hundreds of book bags and supplies annually. She trains youth in sexual purity and home economics, culminating in a purity ball annually. She is passionate about the homeless and underprivileged. She goes into the community yearly to pray, feed, and clothe the homeless. She also launches campaigns to distribute food at Thanksgiving and toys at Christmas to those in need.

She enjoys reading, arts and crafts, interior decorating, fashion designing, and gardening in her spare time. In the community in which she lives, her yard was awarded the Yard of the Year.

For her commitment to building a stronger community through service and leadership, she is a recipient of numerous awards and honors: Life Time Achievement Award, the Trailblazer Leadership Award, and the Volunteer Award from the President of the United States, Barak Obama; Outstanding Georgia Citizen Award from the Georgia Secretary of State; Charles Lawrence Real Estate Agent of the Year Award; 21st Century Matriarch Award; one of Atlanta's 100 top Women of Influence by the Atlanta Business League; The Trumpet Awards Foundation Award; First Ladies of Excellence Award; The Women of Worth Award; The City of Douglasville Service Award; Viewer's Choice Award for successfully achieving over 100,000 views on any particular social media video; She Is Powerful Inc. Award; Elin Community Development Center Award; LaShana Enrichment Program Award; The Magnanimous Award nominee and more for her dedicated service.

In addition to all she accomplished. Dr. Canion graciously partners in ministry with her husband, the Honorable Bishop Michael Canion. Together, they pastor The Assembly of Truth Ministries. She is the mother of two children, India and Christian, and a proud grandmother.

Made in the USA
Columbia, SC
09 February 2025